Thinking of becoming a Catholic?

by Fr Michael Seed SA

*All booklets are published thanks to the
generous support of the members of the
Catholic Truth Society*

CATHOLIC TRUTH SOCIETY
PUBLISHERS TO THE HOLY SEE

Contents

Taking the road that leads to Rome

The other day I was asked what I would do if someone walked up to me in the street and asked to become a Catholic. "I would advise them immediately to go and see a psychiatrist," I replied. My questioner looked a bit taken aback. I was joking of course, but what I meant was that those who are attracted to the Church are above all seeking wholeness.

Whenever I meet someone who is interested in Catholicism, I try to form a picture of their general life: their spiritual life, their emotional life and their working life. You need to see the whole picture, because wholeness and holiness go together. When we are depressed, for example, our spiritual life is not whole. It is really important to get to know people, to become friends with them, because the best common denominator we have is our humanity.

Wholeness

I am convinced that almost everyone who approaches me inquiring about joining the Church has already made their mind up to become a Catholic before they've even uttered a word. Their question is not really "Why should I become a Catholic?" so much as "How do I become a Catholic?"

There's one case that I will never forget. There was a woman who went to Evensong at Westminster Abbey and was so outraged by what she heard in the sermon that she stormed out and marched straight down Victoria Street to Westminster Cathedral. This very formidable woman accosted me in the cathedral piazza and shouted: "I want to become a Catholic!" It was a command. I said: "OK, but I can't do it here and now." So I gave her my number and asked her to visit me. I couldn't have received her then because she wasn't whole at that point; she was angry and upset. She needed to lose the anger, which she did. She was absolutely fine then.

There are, of course, many people who lack that woman's boldness. They find it difficult to make a first contact with the Church. But they needn't despair. They don't have to go straight to a priest. They may have a Catholic friend or family member who they are happier to confide in. And that is fine.

Reasons

There are all kinds of reasons why people are attracted to Catholicism. And the fact that so many of them are trivial shouldn't disturb anyone. The reason people first think of becoming a Catholic is often not the same reason that they will eventually become one and stay one. For example, I've known people to be attracted to the Church simply by seeing the religious habit, or meeting an extremely beautiful nun, or hearing Mozart's *Coronation Mass*. Five minutes in the Brompton Oratory and you think you're with the Pope in Rome. The externals are very important. The beauty of the Mass is external, but it draws people into something deeper.

This is how the "virus", as I call it, enters the system. The person who catches a virus somehow has to come to terms with it. Eventually you go to see a doctor. In other words, you have to take the step of ringing the doorbell and making that first contact with a priest or a lay Catholic. The virus is, of course, God. This spiritual virus enters into us at the moment we are conceived. We spend most of our lives obsessed with it but perhaps not addressing it. But eventually it has to be dealt with.

Everyone must decide when the moment is right for them. I never hurry people. It's vital to leave

God's worrying to God, to allow whatever is to happen to happen naturally. We cannot rush the process of becoming healthy and whole.

Timing

I always remember the case of dear Fr Harold Riley, an eminent Anglo-Catholic Scripture scholar and theologian, who was received at the age of 92. He entered the Church in the morning and was ordained a deacon in the afternoon. Cardinal Basil Hume ordained him a priest at the Church of Our Lady, Lisson Grove, London a few days later. We think he was probably the oldest candidate for ordination in the world. But when I first approached Cardinal Hume about the possibility of reception and ordination he thought I was crazy.

"You're asking me to ordain a man of 92?" he asked with a raised eyebrow. "The Vatican will think I've gone mad."

"Well, Father, they think you are insane anyway," I replied rather naughtily.

After his ordination Fr Riley lived as a Catholic priest and hermit for the last eight years of his life. He died a few months short of his 100th birthday.

Some people are received into the Church much more quickly. I confess that I once met an Anglican priest at 4pm for tea and by 5.30 pm he left a Roman Catholic. I received him in the crypt of Westminster

Cathedral and got the doorman of Archbishop's House to be his sponsor. I emphasise that this was an extremely unusual occurrence and that I had known the priest well for quite some years. He was no longer a vicar in a parish and he had wanted to be received a long time before that. When we got back from the crypt our tea was still warm and we celebrated with a slice of cake.

The moral of these stories is that there is no ideal time to be received. It varies from person to person. But you will know when the time is right for you.

Joining the 'Sacred College of Oddities'

———⊷⊷⊷———

I always advise people who are thinking of becoming Catholic to "learn on the job". I urge them to go to Mass, preferably on a Sunday. The ideal scenario is for them to attend their local parish church. But in big cities like London they might feel more comfortable going to the cathedral or a religious house, and that is perfectly all right.

Where to start

There's no need to worry about what to do or say during Mass. They should simply let God be God, and just observe and participate as best they can. If they are from an Anglican background much of the Mass will be immediately familiar to them. But I remember meeting one young man who, amazingly, had never heard the word "Jesus" before. He was from a very secular Scandinavian family and had never had any religion in his life. So he was beginning from the beginning. He started going to

Mass and was eventually baptised. Bizarrely, he is now a Lefebvrist.

I find that some potential Catholics get carried away and want to read everything about the Church. That is unnecessary. The most important thing to study is the Creed, which is the perfect summary of our faith. That's the only thing, more or less, that you assent to when you become a Catholic. You simply recite the Creed. Then there's a little sentence: "I believe and profess all that the holy Catholic Church believes, teaches, and proclaims to be revealed by God." The only person who ever supplemented that was Ann Widdecombe, who added, "And the Magisterium, and the Pope and all his successors!" for good measure. Anglo-Catholics, in particular, sometimes know too much, and we have to encourage them to focus on the simple truths of the faith. They often think that if the Pope says good morning it's a weather forecast, or that if the Pope drinks Bavarian wheat beer then they also have to drink wheat beer. But that's not the case. They can drink any kind of beer they like.

Basic reading

It's impossible to learn everything, but it is good to read the classic *Penny Catechism*, or the more recent *Compendium of the Catechism of the Catholic Church*. I encourage people to keep these in their pockets or handbags as they move around. Of course, there are people who do feel compelled to go through the *Catechism* in minute detail. For example, there was a certain MP who bought the new *Catechism* and every Thursday we would go through a different section of it together. That was what he needed. At the start he was in favour of abortion and euthanasia, but he changed on both of those subjects. That wasn't so much because he was persuaded by the Catechism's arguments, but because he recognised the need for authority and obedience. He saw that God was the Chief Whip and that he needed to get in line.

Communion

It's important that those thinking of becoming Catholic don't receive Holy Communion when they go to Mass until they actually become Catholics. This can be painful, but there is a deep reason for it. The Eucharist is the food of the community. It is the food of unity, not the food of division. In St John's Gospel Jesus prayed that they all may be one, not that all may be many. The whole point of the Christian community is to be one. And it is only through sin, hypocrisy and horror that we are not one. Holy Communion is the most sublime sacrament of unity. Therefore it is a contradiction for someone who isn't a Roman Catholic, and who isn't in full communion

I Believe (The Apostles' Creed)

I believe in God, the Father almighty, creator of heaven and earth. I believe in Jesus Christ, his only Son, our Lord. He was conceived by the power of the Holy Spirit and born of the Virgin Mary. He suffered under Pontius Pilate, was crucified, died, and was buried. He descended to the dead. On the third day he rose again. He ascended into heaven, and is seated at the right hand of the Father. He will come again to judge the living and the dead. I believe in the Holy Spirit, the holy Catholic Church, the communion of saints, the forgiveness of sins, the resurrection of the body, and the life everlasting. Amen.

RCIA Rite of Reception

It is my sincere and considered conviction that God is asking me to become a member of the Catholic Church. I believe in what the Catholic Church holds and teaches, and I hope to grow in my faith and understanding. I wish to shape my life in accordance with the teaching of Jesus Christ expressed through the life of the Catholic Church.

A text which is also sometimes used reads:

I believe and profess all that the Magisterium of the Catholic Church believes, teaches and proclaims.

with us, to receive Holy Communion in a Catholic church. There are, admittedly, exceptions to this rule, which the Bishops of England and Wales set out in their teaching document *One Bread, One Body*.

Church of sinners

When I urge people to go to Mass, I feel that I also have to give a health warning. I say that, by and large, our Liturgy can be dire. Our music can be terrible. Our sermons can be uninspiring. But I also tell them not to judge by externals. You may, for example, go to a Mass in California celebrated by a priest who looks like Jesus the surfer, with long, spiky blonde hair and Bermuda shorts. He might have a loaf of bread and some form of alcohol. Even though I don't approve of that in any sense, that priest believes that this loaf of bread and that alcohol will become the Body and Blood of Jesus Christ. He believes this in exactly the same way that Pope Benedict XVI believes it when he celebrates Mass, in the proper and correct way, in St Peter's Basilica. Both of those priests believe in the Real Presence of Christ. That's the beauty of Catholicism, in spite of some liturgical aberrations and low standards of celebration.

When I went to Mass for the first time the church reeked of alcohol. Half the congregation was drunk, and the other half was saying the rosary during Mass. The priest was grumpy and odd. He didn't preach, but just told people off. I wasn't put off at all. On the contrary, I was struck by the thought that here was a Church of sinners, a Church that accepts everything. Everyone finds their home in the Church. We can have Adolf Hitler and Mother Teresa, Oscar Wilde and St Francis, Mae West and St Benedict. When someone becomes a Catholic, I congratulate them by saying: "Welcome to the Sacred College of Oddities." For that is truly what we are.

On the threshold
of the Church Universal

———

*T*he Church commands us to receive people gently and with no element of triumphalism. We are simply helping a fellow traveller to the grave to live out their Christian faith as Roman Catholics. It is all God's work, not ours. The triumph is God's.

Reception

The actual ritual is minute. All that a candidate has to do is to recite the Creed and say one little sentence at the end. Usually they are then confirmed: the gift of the Holy Spirit is given to them.

Traditionally, reception takes place at the Easter Vigil, at the summit of the liturgy and of the Church's faith. It is an awesome experience. For shy people, though, it can be a bit daunting. There are people who simply cannot cope with groups and the *Rite of Christian Initiation of Adults* (RCIA) therefore isn't appropriate for them.

I realise that this can present a real problem for the parish priest. What I suggest is that the priest introduces the person in question to a family or an individual who can guide them quietly. It is best to be received publicly, because becoming a Catholic is not a private act. But, if there is a good reason why this is impossible, people can be received in a private ceremony. It's nothing to do with privilege. It's about personality and circumstance.

RCIA groups

I fully understand why some priests gather everyone – both those seeking baptism and those who are already Christians – into a single RCIA group. These days many clergy are being worked to death, especially if they've got nursing homes, schools and hospitals to look after as well. The one great beauty of the RCIA is community. It allows people to make friends and to get to know one another. Our cathedral RCIA group has people from all over London. Many of them come because they don't belong anywhere else. One member of our group has a doctorate in Divinity from Oxford. It was right for him to join the RCIA course because he needed to belong to a little community.

It's often difficult for those who are leading RCIA courses to find the right level, because in a single group you might have a devout life-long Anglican and a young Asian woman who is discovering Christianity for the first time. Usually very well qualified people are immensely humble and they put up with the slow progress. We can always learn, however much we know.

RCIA courses start around September and meet every week until the Easter Vigil (around April usually). You make a decision around early January to be received. Often groups continue to meet afterwards, usually from May to June. That's fine. And many actually miss the group afterwards because they form a community in a very lonely modern society. But I sometimes think that the RCIA course is a bit too long for very busy people.

I encourage parishes to start in the middle of January and finish at the Vigil. The teaching between September and Christmas is, anyway, very initial. It's important to realise that the RCIA comes out of a missionary context. In some non-Christian cultures it can take as long as four years to complete because candidates have to learn so much from scratch. But because of the absolute rat race in the West, I think it's best to limit the course to three to six months. The RCIA is good, but it needs to be adaptable.

Humility

RCIA courses are led by either a priest or a lay catechist. The most important thing a catechist needs is the right heart. They need to be humble, friendly and open-minded. They must have the honesty to say: "I've been asked to run this group. I'm called a catechist, but I don't know everything. There are some of you here who will know more than I do. I'm sorry if this is painful for you. Perhaps the most beautiful thing is that we are here together, that we can talk, and get to know one another. You are all extremely welcome. The Lord has led you here, and I am here to help you in whatever way I can. If it's God's will for you to be received, you will be."

If this were said at the beginning of every RCIA group, it would put everyone at ease. It doesn't matter if the catechist isn't a born teacher; they can simply read something out to the group or put on one of the excellent catechetical videos that are available nowadays. Half the session should consist of teaching, and the other half of an informal chat with a cup of tea and a biscuit. If catechists don't know the answer to a question they should promise to look it up and come back with the answer the following week.

In my experience it's extremely rare for people to have second thoughts about becoming a Catholic after they have completed the RCIA course and are about to be received. That's because this is God's work. The virus, as I described it earlier, has been in them for a long time. They have made their mind up and are ready to become members of the Church Universal.

The breathtaking freedom of the Church

People sometimes expect to feel radically different after they've been received into the Church. This is often true of those who have just been baptised. But those who were already committed Christians are more likely to feel a sense of continuity. They have been received into full communion with the Catholic Church. They have reached the very nature and essence of the Christian community. They are now members of the One, Holy, Catholic and Apostolic Church. And they continue with their communion with whatever they were formerly.

Continuity and fullness

They don't cease to be Anglicans or Methodists or Quakers. I have never ceased, ever, to be a member of the Salvation Army or a Strict and Particular Baptist. I was baptised at 15, and that's not nonsense. I was going to be a Baptist minister, and that's not nonsense either. If I was an Anglican priest, or a deacon or bishop, these things were not rubbish. They are all beautiful signs of God's grace. Catholicism embraces all the previous states of your life.

How is that possible? Because Jesus founded only one Church. He didn't make Anglicans, or Baptists or Quakers. Denominations are the result of human failure, horror and the abuse of power by all of us, including Catholics. In the ceremony of reception you embrace in a unique way every denomination, because Christ is present, in some way, in all denominations. Becoming a Catholic restores the wholeness of Christianity. It may sound odd, but I feel that I'm living out the spirituality of the Salvation Army and the Baptist tradition more as a Catholic than I ever did as a Salvationist and a Baptist.

Freedom

If there is one word that encapsulates what people feel after they have been received, it is "freedom". They understand that they now belong to one Church and are universal people. They are absolutely and totally free. It puts me in mind of that great (though partly untrue) film 'Braveheart', where Mel Gibson and his men shout "Freedom!" as they charge into battle against the English. They all get wiped out, of course, but there's a great spirit of freedom there. I can't stress that word enough.

This freedom comes from the fact that the person has surrendered. They have surrendered to God, surrendered to themselves, and surrendered the idea (which is very widespread these days) that every single person is infallible except the Pope. So many people believe that each human is infallible, a law unto themselves and answerable to no one. But as Catholics we no longer see the Church or the Pope as something that robs us of our free will. Now we learn to see the papacy as freedom, as a centre of love and guidance, and as a tremendous centre of wisdom. We may not always agree with the Church on many difficult and sensitive issues. That's OK. We are not robots. We are not living under a totalitarian regime, as some would have us believe.

The important thing is to assent to the fact that we could be wrong, to always be willing to look at our life again. If we have difficulties with Church teaching, we must humbly ask the question: "Could I be wrong?" The difficulties that I had when I became a Roman Catholic are not resolved, but I've surrendered them. I've surrendered them to the fact that I don't understand everything. And I'm happy always to listen and to learn. If the Cardinal says something, I will listen to it. If I have difficulty with it, I feel comfortable enough to communicate that difficulty. At the same time, I must be loyal to being in communion. I am in communion, ultimately, with the successors of the Apostles. The Apostles had their differences. St Peter and St Paul had very serious and sincere differences, but both of them strove for unity and for reconciliation.

I stress that this new sense of freedom is not the infantile feeling of having handed over responsibility for our lives to someone else. I haven't surrendered my senses, or my bank balance, or my house, or my telephone bills, but somehow so many things don't matter anymore.

If I am Anglo-Catholic, I don't have to worry any longer about questions of the Real Presence of Our Lord in the Eucharist. I don't have to fret about my devotion to Our Lady or about the use of incense, vestments and statues.

If I've come from the evangelical Anglican tradition, or a Methodist or Baptist background, I'm now free in my biblical scholarship. I'm free to live an evangelical and simple sense of the Gospel of Christ. I no longer have to put up with the liberal interpretation of Scripture and constantly fight to preserve biblical integrity, because the Catholic Church is splendid in its defence of the integrity of Scripture.

If I am middle Anglican, or an affirming Catholic Anglican, my intellect is not lost. I'm now part of a communion that holds academia as a prize gem. For the learned people, we are not brain dead.

If I am artistic or scientific, I belong to a communion that is open to science, to art, to music, all leading to the beauty and the supreme intelligence of God.

Daily struggle

Those who are received into the Church shouldn't worry unduly if they do not instantly become saints. It's natural that they will continue to struggle to live the good life. I recall that Archbishop Desmond Tutu once wrote to me, saying: "I wonder what we would do if we found Adolf Hitler or Idi Amin in heaven, them having found God's love so irresistible?" That's my view of the moral question in our Church. There is a home for everyone. There are, however, rules. And it is God who is our final judge.

Jesus has given all authority in heaven and on earth to the Church. Therefore the wisdom and guidance of the Church is sacred and divine. The Church is also very, very, very human. The freedom that one receives in terms of morality is often hard. But remember that Jesus does not expect us to become saints instantly, in a blinding flash of light. Rather, he wants us to work at becoming saints, slowly and steadily, in our ordinary, everyday lives.

Compendium of the Catechism of the Catholic Church

"The *Compendium*, which I now present to the Universal Church, is a faithful and sure synthesis of the *Catechism of the Catholic Church*. It contains, in concise form, all the essential and fundamental elements of the Church's faith, thus constituting, as my Predecessor had wished, a kind of *vademecum*, which allows believers and non-believers alike to behold the entire panorama of the Catholic faith."

Benedictus PP XVI

ISBN: 1 86082 376 9

CTS Code: Do 742

Informative Catholic Reading

We hope that you have enjoyed reading this booklet.

If you would like to find out more about CTS booklets - we'll send you our free information pack and catalogue.

Please send us your details:

Name ....

Address ....

....

....

Postcode ....

Telephone...

Email ....

Send to: CTS, 40-46 Harleyford Road,
            Vauxhall, London
            SE11 5AY

Tel: 020 7640 0042
Fax: 020 7640 0046
Email: info@cts-online.org.uk